The SIGNIFICANCE FACTOR

5 STEPS TO DISCOVERING AND CREATING A LIFETIME LEGACY

The SIGNIFICANCE FACTOR
5 STEPS TO DISCOVERING AND CREATING A LIFETIME LEGACY

EBONI L. TRUSS

THE SIGNIFICANCE FACTOR
Published by Purposely Created Publishing Group™

Copyright © 2015 Eboni L. Truss

ALL RIGHTS RESERVED.

No part of this book may be reproduced, distributed or transmitted in any form by any means, graphics, electronics, or mechanical, including photocopy, recording, taping, or by any information storage or retrieval system, without permission in writing from the publisher, except in the case of reprints in the context of reviews, quotes, or references.

Printed in the United States of America

ISBN (ebook): 978-1-942838-35-7
ISBN (paperback): 978-1-942838-34-0

Special discounts are available on bulk quantity purchases by book clubs, associations and special interest groups.
For details email: sales@publishyourgift.com
or call (888) 949-6228.

For information logon to:
www.PublishYourGift.com

DEDICATION

This book is dedicated to my sons, Gabriel Jaimz and Michael Jacob, and to my husband, James. Gabe and Lou, I pray that of all the people I have intentionally impacted, positively affected, and poured my life into, you two are the *most* impacted. I watch you and wonder why God decided to entrust me with helping to "train you up in the way that you should go," but at the same time, I am honored that I was chosen to be your mommy. I wouldn't have had it any other way. I love you inexplicably.

James, you have been more than a husband to me. You have been the husband *for* me. I do not believe there is anyone else on the planet who is better equipped by God to deal with me, stand by me, or support me. Our "ups and downs" have been just that—*ours*—and my life is the better for it. When I am away from you, my heart aches, and when you're near, I am the happiest. You have walked alongside me (sometimes with teeth clenched) as I traversed my layers of breakthrough. This "new" me, this woman who has found her significance beside you, is your reward. Thank you from the bottom of my heart.

TABLE OF CONTENTS

Dedication		v
Acknowledgements		ix
Preface		vx
Introduction: You Don't Matter		1
Chapter 1	In Search of Significance	5
Chapter 2	Deciding You Matter	15
Chapter 3	Greatness Defined	29
Chapter 4	Going in the Direction of Greatness	55
Chapter 5	What is Your Evidence?	81
Chapter 6	The Man in the Mirror	107
Chapter 7	Power of Agreement	111
About the Author		117

ACKNOWLEDGEMENTS

Lord, You are amazing! Never in my wildest imagination did I ever expect to be an author, let alone a bestselling one! Your direction is the only reason this work exists. Thank you for giving me the words that help to change lives. It is an honor to be used by You and a privilege to know You. My prayer is that You will use this book as a midwife to each reader for generations to come. I love You. Thank You Father.

James, Gabe, and Michael, you have sacrificed so much. I don't think anyone really has a clue how much you guys actually have had to give up as I serve my gifts to the world. No word of thanks is adequate to express how much I relied on your patience while I was up late working, forgot bedtime stories, and ALL the times you heard, "Shhh! I'm on a call!" My life is so much richer because you three are in it. I owe you so much, and I love you so much more. You are my favorite fellas. Thank you, my sons, for being so sweet to your mommy. Thank you, James, for loving me through and through.

To my Momma and my brother, Jason, thank you for reminding me that I was once an incessant writer, thus the gift never left. Because of you, I am now a bestselling author. Thank you for holding me accountable to my success and my significance.

To my BFF, LeMeika Marks, thank you for keeping me grounded. There are times when you believe in me more than I believe in myself, and that level of support can only come from a true and genuine friendship. You are not only my best friend, but you are indeed my sister; blood couldn't make us any closer. Thank you for knowing so much about me yet loving me anyway.

I am blessed to be able to call Minister Yakinea Marie Duff my mentor. You have not only allowed me to stand beside you, but you have also encouraged me to stand on your proverbial shoulders and exercise my own power and genius. Your life gives me the courage to live my own out loud. You are a shining example of what it means to be living on purpose. Your gentle nudges to "get the book done" helped me to see the light at the end of the journey. Thank you for your support and your love.

To my coach, Aprille Franks-Hunt, my resident "Super Star, famous person!" You were the one who first gave me the platform to become an author, alongside 27 other beautiful women, in our bestselling book, *Fabulous New Life*. In doing so, you also gave me the courage and push I needed to put pen to paper for this work. When you responded, "You really should!" after I shared that I wanted to write a solo project, you helped to ignite the spark that has become *The Significance Factor*. Thank you for believing in my significance.

To the women I served with as a part of Iota Chi Kappa (IXK) Christian Sorority, Inc, I owe a huge debt of gratitude. My transition from service with the organization to service in the world has had its bumps, twists, and turns. However, even in my mistakes, you all were still patient, supportive, loving, and kind. I would not trade any of you, and I love you very much! Thank you for following an imperfect leader and helping me to understand that perfection was not a requirement in the first place.

To Nicole Hutchinson Henningham, Brittaney Pleasant, Sequoia Gillyard, and Takima Howze, thank you for paving the way before me as published authors. Each of your works stands as a testament to the faithfulness of God to His people and to your purpose. Thank you for being an example of what's possible to those who believe!

Keithra Morley, your consistency in keeping me mindful of the goal is unmatched. You have been as excited about this book coming to fruition as I have. I thank God for you and the accountability you have provided. Thank you for believing in me and saying so!

I am convinced that I have the BEST coaching clients in the known world! My clients and my community rock like grandma's chair, and I LOVE it! Thanks to each of you for your feedback, your honesty, and your participation in my coaching programs, free trainings, live events, and of course, for investing in this book. I am humbled and honored that you continue to allow me to serve you. Thank you for trusting me with your missions and your visions.

To you, the reader, I want you to know that you can be legendary. Regardless of your age, your socioeconomic status, your location, or your relationship status, you are only a decision away from recognizing your greatness. Thank you for allowing me to guide you on this journey.

PREFACE

If your desire is to discover and articulate your worth, purpose, and significance because you want to live a life that is effective and impacting, then this book was written just for you. Within these pages, I outline and detail the steps to uncover your *Significance Factor* by pulling back the layers of decision, definition, dissection, direction, and domination so that you can live a breathtaking life and, as a result of your death, leave a tremendous legacy that spans generations.

I need to warn you though—this book may be a bit of a shock to you. I may even come across as cynical at times or far too nonchalant about the conversation we're having. Other times, I will step on your proverbial toes, and you will feel uncomfortable. That *is* my intention. I want to challenge you—make you angry even so that you'll finally make the decisions necessary to change the life you are currently leading. Everything in life begins with a decision. Today is your day of reckoning.

The Significance Factor

What's most important to me is that this book gets in the hands of every person who wants to do more than just live to die. They want to *matter*. Instead of a period at the end of their life, they want an ellipsis, signifying that they have poured into others; therefore, they live on, all over the earth. Mind you, I don't mean proverbially or esoterically. I mean creating a life that has literally and strategically impacted and affected so many other lives that individuals can trace their success and impact right back to you. That is the effect legendary people have. They are more than just an obituary in the family photo album. They are the subject of writings, speeches, museums, statues, and works of art.

I invite you to take the steps necessary to join their ranks.

INTRODUCTION

"A life is not important except in the impact it has on other lives." – Jackie Robinson

YOU DON'T MATTER!

Yup. I said it. I just confirmed what you have been thinking for months, years, possibly even decades. You don't matter—your life, your personal accomplishments, or your voice. If you died today, would the world be affected? Would there be anyone outside of your family who could or would say that they are different because you lived? That their life was impacted infinitely because of you? Or, at your death, after your funeral, will you just become another obituary in the family photo album?

"My life is my message." – Mahatma Gandhi

You. Don't. Matter.

Is it jarring? Did it feel like you just swallowed a bolder and it hit the pit of your stomach like an explosion? Do you feel exposed? As if that thing that you've been fighting to hide from is now looking you square in the eye? The truth tends to have that effect. The truth can hurt. Did you say "ouch!" when I told the truth about you my friend? Did you feel as though your "secret" were out? If not, this book is not for you. Congratulations! You can close it now. However, if you are still reading, then you are probably fully aware of your insignificance and are, fortunately, unsatisfied with that. You could have possibly been hoping someone would call you to the carpet. (I tend to have that effect on people.) Or you could have only now realized that your life is, and has been to some degree, insignificant. You could possibly be amazed that you hadn't realized it before now. (I tend to have that effect on people as well.)

Therefore, I feel it only right and necessary that I ask you: Now, faced with the reality of being caught in a life where you don't matter, what do you plan to do? If you don't have an answer, I am elated that you are still holding this book in your hands. It will guide you to your answer—the answer that you've sought after for years or the answer that you never knew you needed until now. You CAN matter. In fact, you're supposed to!

I dare you, my friend, to become legendary...

In Search of Significance

"The two most important days in your life are the day you were born and the day you figure out why."
– Mark Twain

So how do we go about crafting a life where hundreds, thousands, even millions are affected? How do we stand out in life and in death? How do we create a life and death that truly matter in the world? First, let's get clear on our terms. In this text, the term "significance" is meant to denote your personal importance, which covers every aspect of your life and death. "Significance"

can also be interchanged with "purpose" or the divine reason you are on this side of the grass. Consequently, there will be times when we are talking about your personal importance on the planet, but that is with the understanding that you are important on this planet because of your divine purpose.

Let's be clear—whether you know it or not, you are important. The fact that you are breathing is proof of that. Though in order to live a life of significance, the first step is that you must be completely sold on two things:

1. **You were significantly created.**

2. **You have a significant purpose and therefore should live a significant life.**

The challenge that most people have is that they look for the "why" in these assertions as opposed to living in the truth of them. They ask questions like, "Why was I even born?" and "Why does my life have to be so messed up?" They also tell lies like, "I'll never be anything in my life" or "I'm a nobody."

Your birth may be the product of your mother's rape, or you may have been an unexpected or unwanted pregnancy. You may have been abandoned by your parents or never knew your father. As such, you loathe your birth and lament, when really you should be celebrating by saying, "YES! I was born!" Your parents may have been drug addicts, alcoholics, or had some other vice. You may have grown up in the ghetto, so you might feel you don't *deserve* to be seen as significant. You have settled on the erroneous notion that significance, success, and status are for others and not you. Allow me to help you out with that.

In your middle school sex education class, you were taught that you were one of about four million sperm that vigorously swam to the egg that your mother released. And unless you are a twin, triplet, etc., you were the one who arrived at the egg first. You were the spark that brought life to your mother's womb. Do you realize what that means? That means YOU won! You got there first, you fertilized the egg, YOU WON! Please catch the gravity of your conception and birth! The fact that you were born, that you *won*, means that winning has been in your nature before you hit the planet! Not only were you *born* a winner, but you have *always* been a winner. It doesn't matter what you were born into, why you were born into it, or whether or not you should have been. The fact is that YOU ARE A WINNER, and it is in your very DNA to win! Breathe that in for a second...

> ***The story currently around your conception and birth doesn't matter; you have ALWAYS been a winner!***

You were significant in your creation, and you have to reconcile that in your own heart and mind. You have to relish in it and celebrate it! Otherwise, creating a legendary life and death will be impossible. You will NEVER be able to convince other people of what you are not convinced of yourself.

Second, you have to become completely aware and confident of your significant purpose. You must decide and agree that you have a significant purpose, therefore, you should live a significant life. If no one outside your sphere of influence knows your name and what you do, you don't really have the influence and significance that you were born to have! The reality is, *your gift should be making room for you*. If it is not, then you haven't made a quality decision yet. You have to decide to live your significance out loud!

In August 2008, I was also at that place of decision. At that time, my son Gabriel and I were involved in a terrifying vehicle accident. While on the highway traveling to a neighboring city, a woman pulled out into oncoming traffic in order to cross to the other side of the highway. Of course my first instinct was to swerve to miss her. Had I hit her mini-van, the impact would have instantly killed her and quite possibly her children inside. But in swerving my SUV, I sent my son and I (he was four-years-old at the time) back and forth across the two-lane highway twice and onto the median where we flipped three times and landed upside down. I don't remember much of the action of that day, only that I was thinking, "I have got to keep this car in the road because my baby is in the back seat..."

At the scene, my only concern was my son—getting him out of the toppled vehicle, getting him home, and making sure he was not traumatized. I believe at some point, I either went into shock or into survival mode. Instead of attempting to contact my husband, I was thinking through how Gabe and I were going to get home and what I was going to do about a car. I had to get to work the next day! There were several drivers who had witnessed the accident and stopped their cars on the highway to help with the rescue efforts. (I can only imagine what it was like to watch an SUV swerve across a highway and then flip down the middle of it!) Their expectation was that we were either severely injured or worse. Although the enemy's plan was that either my son or I, or both, be killed in that accident, because of the mercy of God and His protection, neither scenario played out. Both my son and I left the scene unscathed.

God is Awesome!

The next day, and for many days after, I thought about that car accident. I played the events over and over in my mind, trying to remember more than what I could. Then, it suddenly dawned on me that I could have died that day. I hadn't thought about that before. I mulled over that and then considered the implications. One thought constantly crossed my mind: If I had died that day, would anyone have been impacted besides my husband and my mother? Would there have been anyone who could say that his or her life was different because I had lived?

See, I understand where you are right now because my unfortunate answer was also "no," and I didn't like that. In all honesty, I made myself angry. I was outraged by the life that I was *not* leading as a result of living beneath my privilege and my purpose. The truth was that I had not significantly impacted anyone beyond my immediate circle. (And whether I had impacted my immediate circle *significantly* was questionable!) The fact of the matter was, my life, until that point, had been incredibly insignificant. I had not shown up in the world at all. That is why you are holding this guide in your hands. Not long after that accident, I had the "aha" moment—I made the decision that I was significantly created and should be living a significant life. Now it's your turn!

You may have survived a traumatic experience. For you, it may have been a car accident as well, or it could have been surviving cancer, being raped, or living with being abandoned at birth. Your mother or father may have just died, or you may have suffered the death of your child. Maybe you're "just" a stay-at-home mom (or dad) or "just" working to pay the bills. You may be middle-aged and single with no prospects and fearful that you'll have no legacy to leave. Regardless of the situation you find yourself in, the beautiful thing is that you've finally found yourself. And that, my friend, is what matters.

Significant Questions

When is your birthday? _____

Before reading the first chapter, how did you feel about that day?

_____

_____

_____

After reading chapter one, have your feelings changed?   Yes   No

How so or why not?

_____

_____

_____

What have you decided about your life? (Hint: Think about the two things I mention in chapter one.)

_____

_____

_____

What is it that you want from your life?

1. _____

2. _____

3. _____

Will you use the steps in this guide to help you create that life? YES. YES!!!!

Deciding You Matter

"Everybody is a genius. But if you judge a fish by its ability to climb a tree, it will live its whole life believing that it is stupid." — Albert Einstein

Once you have made the quality decision that you were born to be and do something significant in the world, the next step is to define what your personal significance is. My question to you then becomes, "Who are YOU?" Most often when asked that question, people begin running down their titles: mother, teacher, entrepreneur, doctor, little league coach, motivational speaker, executive director, PTA president—the list can go on and on. But really to respond with a title is cheating; it does not allow for those around you to know who the real you is. Furthermore, naming all your titles doesn't allow YOU to see YOU for who you really are. Titles are the hiding places of the insignificant. Let me rephrase my question:

Who are you, *outside* of your titles?

In working with my coaching clients all across the country, I have found a bit of a running theme—we're in an unspoken competition with the "Joneses" (or the Smiths, or the Johnsons, or the Walkers... you get the idea). For various reasons, we feel we're not enough, so we try to do more stuff to get more titles and be more important than Mrs. Jones. Amazingly, Mrs. Jones is so sold on her own purpose and personal importance that she couldn't care less about your title, and further, she is oblivious to the competition! It amounts to you being the only rat in the race. Your concern with Mrs. Jones's importance has caused you to deny your own!

Olympic swimmers and world class chefs

Imagine you were born to win in swimming, so much so that you qualified to compete in the Olympic Games. You trained incredibly hard, for hours on end, in the pool and in the gym or wherever your coach instructed you to be. Now imagine further that I am your friend who was born to win at cooking. I am an AH-MAYZING connoisseur of all things cuisine. I begin to share with you my phenomenal recipes, and you love them! I begin getting opportunities to travel the country, get a scholarship to the top cooking school, and I become a world-class chef. As life continues, I get featured on television shows and meet celebrities. My life has morphed into this *beautiful* thing! In the meantime, you're still in the pool prepping for the Olympic Games. You begin to think it's unfair that I am getting all the kudos. After all, you're going to be an Olympian for goodness sake! Don't you deserve some credit? Shouldn't there be some sort of accolade for you as well?

The Significance Factor

Did you see what just happened? You had your eyes on the kitchen when they should have been on the pool! Consequently, your attitude changed; you went from being an Olympian to "just a swimmer." The problem with that is you are comparing yourself to someone who isn't even in your lane (no pun intended). Too often we trick ourselves into believing that our preparation during our journey must be the same as another person's. Worse yet, we are steeped in the fallacy that we are competing against each other for attention and praise. Our ignorance causes us to consider that our *title* must be equally important to the next person's or our efforts are in vain. What we need to realize is that our journey belongs to us. It is unique to us and is as unique as we each are. You cannot compare your preparation in the pool to my preparation in the kitchen. It's not fair, and it's not feasible. We each have our own journey. My only role in yours is to cheer you on and support you when needed, and vice versa.

What I want you to understand right here, my friend, is that you are in competition with NO ONE. That's right, there is no one like you, there has never been anyone like you, and there will never be anyone like you. Period. (Where I'm from they'd say, "Point blank, period!") I encourage you, therefore, to stop working to get more titles so that you can feel significant. The title does not give you importance; you give importance and merit to the title.

There is another category within "titles" that I see many women chasing—"Mrs." I have encountered many women who are so enamored of the title "Mrs." that they are willing to, and subsequently do, settle in a relationship with any man who will give them the time of day. They then have to contend with a life that is mediocre, detrimental, and oftentimes, physically and/or emotionally abusive. Listen, love, there is no relationship and no title worth that exchange. Furthermore, there is no MAN worth that! You and only you can define who you are, your personal significance, and your divine purpose. You will not "find yourself" in a man or any other relationship. Adding "Mrs." before your name will not bring about that sort of revelation. Only an honest assessment of your life, some soul searching, and living in truth can do that.

Jane, Janet, and the Jet Setters

My entire life, for as far back as I can remember, I have wanted to be an attorney. I vacillated on the type of law I wanted to practice, but I never wavered on my decision to practice law in some form. Everyone who knew me knew that about me, and fortunately, my mom allowed me to participate in opportunities to help me plan my career. I settled on corporate law, specifically acquisitions and mergers. I wanted to jet set and fly around the world overseeing the buying and selling of major companies. I had carefully constructed my life and anticipated being single at least until I was 30 years old. I had a world to see after all.

During my junior year at Talladega College, I began gathering applications for the law schools I had considered attending: Pennsylvania State, Columbia University, Howard University, Cumberland School of Law, and Carnegie Mellon. At one point, I was sitting in my dorm room with the applications strewn all across my bed as I asked God which school He wanted me to attend. The problem was that I had never once asked the Lord if I was supposed to attend law school or even if I was supposed to practice law at all. Imagine my surprise when the Lord answered by saying matriculation through law school was not what He intended for me. And although I had an inclination that He wanted me to be involved in some sort of full-time Christian service, I found that He did not want me to attend seminary either. In fact, His plan was that I remain in Talladega, AL! I was devastated. Here I was, a junior in college, with the pressure to "make something" of myself, and now I had no plan. What's worse is that I also could not return home to Detroit.

Fast forward a few years and I am still living in Talladega, AL, now married with a son. I have become an elementary school teacher and lead a pretty average (insignificant) life. I'm a late adopter to this "new" social media phenomenon, Facebook, and after joining, I accepted the friend requests from several of my college buddies. Two of them in particular, we'll call them Jane and Janet, had become quite successful. In fact, they were living the "jet setter" life that I had always planned, and they posted the pictures that proved it. I'd find myself obsessing over their timelines wishing I were them and not "just a teacher." They were making the money, the moves, and the magic that I was supposed to be making. I would intimate to my husband that I felt too "regular," like I hadn't accomplished anything in life. What I didn't recognize at the time was that those feelings were really just my purpose calling to me; my time of being insignificant was drawing to a close. Can you relate?

In the years that followed, between wishing I were Jane or Janet and actually realizing my true significance, I tried to embark upon other careers or avenues. At the time, I thought they had truly become genuine interests. Several *new* career desires and passions began to surface: joining the Marine Corp (to which my husband thought I had gone mad), becoming a United States Marshal, studying civil engineering, participating in more multilevel marketing opportunities than I care to remember, three different stints as a Mary Kay Consultant, and even pursuing a doctoral degree in education. I was looking for significance in all the wrong places. I wanted to *feel* important, like I had accomplished something, so that I wouldn't *feel* so regular, so unaccomplished, and insignificant.

I'm sure by now you can guess why I was devastated in college and wasted time obsessing over Jane and Janet's lives as a young adult—I had associated significance with titles, degrees, and money. In my world, your significance was attached to these three things. While that does have some truth (those with money and resources tend to have the most influence), the reality is that significance is not predicated upon a yearly income, a net worth, or a title. Think about Mother Teresa. I would guess that she is one of the most well-known women to ever live and has been for generations. However, she took a vow of poverty and committed her life to serving mankind. She successfully rallied people with money and resources behind her cause and will live forever in history as a champion of the poor, sick, and destitute. Why? I believe it is because she recognized early on that before she was a nun (title), she was a *servant* (person). She was a mouthpiece for those who had no voice of their own. She recognized her purpose and her significance. If she were to have never become a nun, I am willing to bet she still would have been a servant, a mouthpiece. She could articulate who she was sans titles, and therefore, would have lived her significance out loud regardless, without hesitation or apology. What will you do my friend?

Significant Questions

What are three of your greatest strengths? (Be specific.)

1. _____

2. _____

3. _____

Tell me about one of the biggest challenges you've had in your life. How did you overcome it?

_____

_____

_____

Tell me about your **first** achievement. Don't worry about if it seems boring or "small."

_____

What are some **unusual** skills that you have?

_____

_____

_____

What would not be the same had you NOT been a part of it (e.g. a project, event, work, or volunteer effort)?

_____

_____

_____

_____

What do you get complimented on the most?

___

___

___

What do you like most about yourself?

___

___

___

Taking all your responses into account, who would you now say YOU are, outside of your titles?

___

___

___

Greatness Defined

"It is literally true that you can succeed best and quickest by helping others to succeed."
— Napoleon Hill

You have made the necessary, quality decision. Check. You have also defined your significance. Check. However, there is still work to be done. Your third step is to define and design how you will live these realities out. Now we must do the work that it takes to make these foundational pieces more than just "aha" moments. And although ideal, it's highly improbable that you'll wake up tomorrow automatically *being* who you were born to be and living in your significance. You have too much history and too much baggage for the change to be instantaneous; therefore, we have to prepare for it. We have to create a plan of action to help ensure that your significance sees the light of day.

Everything about your life from this day forward must be intentional!

Remember the end goal: creating a *legendary* life and death. You will NOT end up as just another obituary in the family photo album. Your wings called—your time of being a caterpillar has ended.

Let us then begin by dissecting your significance. In order to have a legendary life and death, your significance must be four things: visible, audible, instructional, and measurable. These are crucial pieces of the puzzle that will allow us to build your significance plan; these are your "bricks," if you will.

Visible

The first, and probably most important, brick that you must lay is that of being intentionally **visible**. People form their opinions about you within the first 11 seconds of seeing you. This means that chances are, before you've even had the opportunity to say anything, the individual has already decided your character, how well you do what you do, whether or not you're a crook... you get the idea. So it is crucial that people *see* your significance. That is, you must live the truth of who you are every single day! People need to see you doing *you*. It would be wise then to first determine what they might see.

Oftentimes, we shy away from the "spotlight" for fear that people will think us prideful or arrogant. For others, we shun the exposure because we know that the behavior we continue to indulge in is ethically wrong, out of integrity, or is otherwise immoral (more on that later). However, when our outside is aligned with our inside, people should definitely see that and know that about us. The determining factor is our motive. Are we visible in earnest hope of affecting change for people, or are we simply "showing out" in an effort to be seen? What I believe I know about you is that the former is true; otherwise, you would have stopped reading at the introduction! Therefore, I need for you to clarify in your own heart and mind that you MUST be visible in order to have a legendary life and death. And because your heart is right about what you are doing and attempting to accomplish, people will be attracted to your message. It's almost like magic—the more authentic we are, the more people will see us. We create our own "stage" as it were.

There is another segment of people I need to speak to as well. There are those of you who were once visible and you lived your significance out loud for a season, but now you have become invisible. No one takes notice anymore, but in some ways you're okay with that. It doesn't bother you. I believe this happens not because we intend for it to, but because we have become complacent. The "room" that we play in has become too small. As my mom once told me, "You're a big fish in a little pond, and you like it." That's what has happened to you. You have outgrown the "room," but because you are content and safe, you have lost the connection to your significance's need to be visible.

Let's self-assess. You need to be in a bigger room if:

- Everyone in the current room is asking you for direction, but you can't ask any of them for the same.

- Everyone in the current room needs *your* advice, *your* expertise, and/or *your* approval.

- There is no one left for you to serve in the current room, so everyone is trying to serve you.

- You are bored in the current room.

You need to be in a room full of people who make you feel inadequate. Why? So that you'll be challenged to enlarge your territory, your vision, and your scope! That will in turn charge you to become visible again because you'll realize there is still work to be done. Legends never quit. Legends never shrink back. *Legends never die.* Begin today to deliberately seek out bigger rooms where you can get more knowledge on where to take action and where you can serve those around you. And when that room gets "too small," as it absolutely should, don't become satisfied. Immediately seek out the next "bigger room."

Other times, we avoid playing in the bigger room because of low self-esteem or poor self-worth. For many years, I struggled horribly with feelings of inadequacy that led to perfectionism and body image issues. Everyone around me knew I was filled with greatness and brilliance, but I didn't. They were convinced of a truth that I couldn't even convince myself of. For me, the root cause stemmed from various instances of rejection in my childhood (which is often where rejection begins).

As a sixth grader, I had a huge crush on a fellow classmate. In hindsight, it could definitely be described as "puppy love," but as with most sixth grade girls, it felt to me like he was "the one." One afternoon, my mom came to check me out of school early, and my crush just happened to be in the school's main office at the time. Instead of paging my teacher, the school secretary sent my crush back to our classroom with the message that my mom was on campus. When he arrived back to the classroom, instead of walking over to our homeroom teacher and sharing with him the message, my crush said to the entire class, "Eboni, your momma is in the office waiting for you. She is FINE... I don't know *what* happened to you." The silence was deafening. Everyone looked at me to see what I would say in response, but all my energy was focused on holding back the tears that were quickly welling. I had no words. I had no comeback for that blatantly disrespectful insult. I heard a few of his friends snicker and talk amongst themselves. My eyes filled with tears, and I grabbed my belongings and left. I had been crushed by my crush.

In terms of physical attributes, I've never been thin. I've always been "the big girl" or the "thick one." I surmised that this was the main reason my sixth grade crush never reciprocated my feelings. It was not long after that incident that I secretly, as a sixth grader, began using diet pills and Slim Fast™ shakes to lose weight. I'd hide them in a lunch bag in my backpack and never truly explained to my friends what the concoction really was. So early on, despite whatever intelligence or capability I may have possessed, I never wanted to be out in front. I never wanted to be seen. I always feared someone making the same observation that my sixth grade crush did: "What happened to *you*?"

I was well into adulthood before I even considered the notion that I am valuable, worthy, and of course, significant. Only then did I begin acknowledging that *I* am a big fish, regardless of the size of the pond or its other inhabitants. Along with awakening to the reality of my own personal significance, I had to deal with and heal from rejection, low self-worth, and even lower self-esteem. I became comfortable with being visible and being seen as I pursued purpose and lived significantly. Now, love, you must do the same. What will people see? Will they see someone who is confident with their head held high? Or will they look upon someone who, with their posture, is apologizing for their existence? Will you be someone who dresses the part, or will you make excuses for mediocrity? Can you afford to continue to play small, or worse yet, not play at all?

What's the status of the room you are currently in? Are you in the *waiting room*—waiting on God, waiting on the "right" time, waiting on the kids to graduate, waiting on something or other to occur? Be mindful that usually what you're professing to be waiting on is usually just a way for you to avoid making the decisions that will lead you to your destiny. If you are a habitual excuse maker and creator, chances are you are in the waiting room, and you will remain there until you take action. No clock that was ever made had a "right" setting for the time, and no calendar has ever included a "one" day. There is only *today*, and in the waiting room, too many "todays" pass you by.

Are you in the *emergency room*? This means you have reached the place where you understand that discovering your significance and living it out loud is a "life or death" situation. Those who are in the emergency room have reached a breaking point. They realize that assistance is necessary, but their willingness to live significantly outweighs their desire to die unnoticed. Those in the waiting room understand that friends and family may become uncomfortable, upset, irritated, or disheartened by the choices being made, while you are determined and undaunted; you WILL be significant in both life and death. Is that you?

You may be one who is in the *play room* because you believe that you have time to spare. You are still trying to "find yourself," or you too are a big fish in a small pond, and you are satisfied with that. The time that you consider to be "spare" is really *wasted* time that you cannot get back. In the play room, you become satisfied with the distractions—the "toys" in your life if you will—which fool you into believing that they are enough and that the pursuit of significance is unnecessary, too time consuming, or just plain too difficult. It is much easier to play around in this mindset.

Or are you in the (just plain) *living room*? It's enough for you to just "make it" every day. Thinking about how to live significantly is just not very high on the overall list of priorities. Your station in the living room resembles international bestselling author, Robin Sharma's chiding when he said, "Don't live the same year 75 times and call it a life." You are complacent, comfortable, and content because you believe that it's much safer to be "regular" than it is to be significant. In the living room, paying your bills, raising your children, and living a "decent" life are all it takes to be happy. Unfortunately, there is much more that needs to be done if you ever plan to be *fulfilled*.

Audible

You also need to be intentionally **heard**. People need to hear you being you. That means that we now need to lay the groundwork for your message. What will you say to the world? After all, there is an audience in the earth that belongs to you. Your journey, no matter what it is and where it's heading, has a story attached. Every moment that you breathe, that story is being crafted to be told to an audience. Just like your significance, your story is unique to you, and no matter where in that story you are currently, you must always be prepared to tell it. Now, that does not necessarily mean you have to show up in the world as a speaker (although that is definitely an option). But it does mean that you should take each opportunity you are presented with to share your story.

Let's revisit Mother Teresa's life. As we've discussed, she came to the realization that her significance was being a champion of and a voice for the less fortunate. Her life's work revolved around that decision, and as a result, we know her name (visibility). At the same time, she was consistently sharing with everyone she could about her mission, from the stranger on the streets of Calcutta, to Parliament, to center floor at the United Nations. She made her significance *heard*. In every circumstance, her message was, "I am here as a representative of the downtrodden, and I need for you to listen to me." She understood that her purpose, her personal importance, necessitated that she not only be seen but that she be heard as well.

Once, I was invited to speak at a women's empowerment conference in Atlanta, Georgia. I was to share the stage with prominent national and international speakers who had far more renown in the space than I did at the time. Not only was I to speak, but the conference host heard the topic I planned to share and asked me to OPEN the conference (cue the jaw drop). Initially, I was so honored that it wasn't until later that I began to hear the voice of insignificance and fear. It tried to convince me that I was not enough to be on the stage with these phenomenal women, let alone be the first speaker. Who did I think I was? And surely the conference host was confused, right? What will the attendees think when they see these "big" names and then my little ol' name on the flyer and website? I went back and forth with that voice for about a week. Then, I had finally had enough. My OWN voice of significance finally began to rise up. When it did, I became even more convinced that the message I was to share needed to be heard. Not only that—I also decided that I was important enough to be the one to share it. I am important enough to be heard.

Some of you were probably waiting for me to say it was the devil who was the voice of insignificance and fear. You may have even imagined the cartoon of a little demon on one of my shoulders and an angel on the other. Not so. The voice of insignificance was mine. It was the attempt of the old baggage to get some attention. It was the effort of other people's fears trying to find a place in my life. That voice of insignificance was the rise of years and years of denial of who I am and years of apology for who God has called me to be.

Do I feel bad about that voice trying to take precedence over the truth? Nope. Why? First, because I handled it without fear. It took a minute—and thankfully it takes less time now—but I beat that voice back with my own audible voice. Second, I don't feel bad because I know I'm not the only one. You've heard that voice too. Some of you from the inside, others from the outside, but I know I'm not alone. Fortunately, we now know about each other, and what's better is that we now know what to do:

When each opportunity comes, speak the truth, even if your voice shakes!

Instructional

When you are intentionally seen and heard, you will eventually begin to gain a following.

Your audience, those who your life is supposed to feed, will begin to reach out to you. They will begin to glean from your wisdom, your experience, and your expertise, first remotely and then personally or one-to-one. Once you have arrived at this leg of your journey, it is vital that as your audience sees you and hears you, they also should be able to follow your example. Your significance must also be intentionally ***instructional***. Whether or not you like it or approve of it, there will be people watching you and basing their behavior on yours. It is the nature of the beast when you make the decision to live your significance out loud and in the open. Consequently, I must now ask you, how will you live? What will be the core values that dictate your behavior?

Let's be clear—the tongue in your mouth has to match the tongue in your shoe. It is not difficult to spot a fake and a hypocrite. All one has to do is watch what he or she does behind "closed doors." That is, do your words match your actions? As I mentioned earlier, some shirk exposure because of what they are doing that they should NOT be. To be fair though, I must say that this can also go another way. When your significance is intentionally instructional, people will flock to you. They will want you to coach them, mentor them, or otherwise speak into their lives somehow. What will you do when that happens? This is important to think through beforehand because it's coming. An instructional life is one that is characterized by integrity and fairness and humility. You must be clear on your commitment to these ideals. If not, you run a tremendous risk of hurting those who have entrusted in you and negatively affecting their personal sense of significance.

About four months into my coaching and speaking career, I met Zenovia White Andrews. She is not only a transformational speaker, coach, author, pastor, and the CEO of the MaxOut Group, Inc., but she is also a multimillionaire, having created massively successful businesses alongside her husband. She is a wonderful spirit; she uniquely and genuinely cares about God's people. I took the opportunity to enroll in one of her coaching programs. With that came the opportunity for a one-on-one call with her. My knees were knocking! I was excited and nervous at the same time. As she listened to me and then coached me through to my next step, I heard the Spirit of God say, "Ask her to be your mentor." I wanted to faint when she agreed without hesitation. I didn't understand until later why I got that direction from the Spirit. Understanding where my husband and I were headed in ministry, business and life, I needed to see, hear, and have the ability to follow someone already living out my future.

Pastor Z (as I like to call her) lives an instructional life. She has invited me into her estate, broken bread with me, spoken into my life, and coached me on many, many things. She is a multimillionaire, but she is approachable and relatable. When she agreed to be my mentor that day, it changed the game for me. I have been taught that a person needs to have more than one mentor in their journey—at least one for each area in which they are lacking expertise, experience, or example. Therefore, Pastor Z is my "Millionaire Mentor." Now, imagine the kind of mentor YOU will be for someone once you have begun living your life to intentionally be an example. Will someone mention your name as an influence in their lives in a book they have written? I hope so.

Measurable

When I am perusing a book at my local bookstore or on Amazon, and I notice your name in it, I'll know it was because you have also made your significance ***measurable***. When your significance is measurable, it means that people are sharing with you and others the impact you have had in their lives. It is a tremendous event when you have individuals who come to you, unsolicited, explaining how something you did or said has changed them for the better, has gotten them back on track, or has otherwise caused them to have a paradigm shift. Take a moment now and think through the lives outside of your family that you have touched. If you cannot readily think of any, that's okay—that's why we're here together. Who and where are the lives you are planning to impact? Think through that.

For the sake of clarification, and in consideration of our society's fascination with social media, we are not calling "likes" and shares as impact. Being YouTube or Facebook "famous" is not what I mean when I say making an impact that will remain after your death. Who are the REAL lives you are impacting, specifically those who would credit you as having a direct influence on who they are as a person? What are these individuals saying about you? Do you want them to be saying more? Then you must do more with and in your significance! Do you want them to be saying something different? Then you need to be living your significance differently!

SIGNIFICANT QUESTIONS

What do people get when they get you? This is not time to be philosophical. Be clear and direct.

_____

_____

_____

What do they see?

_____

_____

What do they hear?

_____

_____

Is your "outside" aligned with your "inside"?
Yes   No

Why not or how so?

_____

_____

What is the status of the "room" you are in currently?

- Waiting Room
- Emergency Room
- Play Room
- (Just) Living Room
- None of these (I'm in the RIGHT room Eboni!)

Explain:

_____

_____

Do you need to immerse yourself in a bigger room?   Yes   No

Why not?

_____

_____

If yes, how will you get to that "bigger" room? What is your plan?

_____

_____

_____

What is your message to the world? What is that ONE thing you want everyone you meet to know?

_____

_____

Who are the people you want to tell this to? (Be specific—"everybody" is too broad)

_____

_____

_____

Are you committed to sharing your stories while delivering your message?   Yes   No

Besides public speaking, in what ways can you make your significance **heard**?

_____

_____

_____

Do you believe you are important enough to be heard?   Yes   No

Why or why not?

_____

_____

_____

Is your life ***instructional***?   Yes   No

Why not or how so?

_____

_____

_____

What is the lesson your life teaches others? (No philosophy here, just specifics!)

_____

_____

What are the core values that dictate your behavior?

_____

_____

_____

How do you plan to handle it when people flock to you? What will you do? How will you respond?

_____

_____

_____

Who are the lives outside of your family that you have impacted or plan to impact?

_____

_____

What do you need to do differently to *immediately* have a greater influence on others?

_____

_____

_____

When will you begin to do this?

_____

_____

Going in the Direction of Greatness

"Efforts and courage are not enough without purpose and direction." – John F. Kennedy

You're ready! You're hyped! You recognize that it's time to live out loud and without apology. You're ready to assume your mission of being seen, heard, and felt. You've committed to living intentionally, creating a life that is also instructional and measurable. YOU FREAKING ROCK! But wait...what's your plan? Who is going to benefit from your mission and your message? Passion and excitement will only take you so far. Your purpose needs direction as much as it needs commitment. Therefore, step four is to dissect your significance. Dissecting your significance is essential if you expect to go any further on this journey. In business we'd call this identifying your target audience or market. I think it's appropriate in this context as well. Think about the point and nature of a target; it gives you focus and a goal to attain. A target allows you to hone in on your activity, making it succinct and powerful. You will burn out like a shooting star if your significance has no direction. While we're here, let's once again define our terms.

For this discussion, we're going to differentiate between the *planet* and the *world*. The *planet* is every human being that is breathing. In my coaching practice, I've had clients who were adamant that their significance and message were for the entire *planet*. Not so. That would be like going to a stadium while a professional sports event was in full swing. Imagine being center court or field, and you're screaming at the top of your lungs to the thousands and thousands of fans who are present. Can anyone hear you? Better still, do they even care? Absolutely not! Imagine if you instead approached two or three rows of seats in the stands and began to share with ONLY those individuals. Do you think your activity would be more effective? You definitely have a better chance. Now, stay with me. If what you had to say was juicy and it would benefit only five or six of the individuals seated in that section of the stands, do you think you'd have a captive audience? You darn skippy! In that moment, you became the center of their *world* and them yours. Aww..."Hercules, Hercules!"

The goal is to speak to your *world* instead of trying to speak to the *planet*. What a beautiful connotation! When you think of those you serve as being your world, it implies that your heart is involved and that there is a commitment—an obligation—that you have to those you serve. Trying to serve the planet will become tiresome and possibly even burdensome. But when you are showing up for your world, it's a joy, and there is always something new to capture!

Time to dissect your significance so we can give it direction. Our focus is on six areas:

1. **Who** lives in your world?

2. **What** are you to do for them/with them/about them?

3. **When** should you start doing it?

4. **Where** on the planet should it be done?

5. **How** will you accomplish it?

6. **Why** does it even matter?

WHO

Who lives in your world? Who is it that you are here to serve your significance to? My world consists of professional women, primarily ages 35-45, who usually work a corporate job but have had an epiphany about their lives. They realize that there is more for them. I like to say that they are "sick and tired of being sick and tired." They are frustrated, unfulfilled, and insignificant in their current lives. This can be for various reasons. Some feel this way because they are not doing in life what they now know they should be doing. Some of them no longer have the emotional fortitude to continue in the same lane they are currently in. They are stressed out completely and no longer have the grace to do what they have been. My world is also filled with women who desire to make a difference in the lives of others. For them, it's not enough to just live to get old. They have to be seen, heard, and felt. They have to become legendary!

What's interesting is that my target audience, the women who make up my world, are much like me! That's why my story is so appealing to them—it's their story as well. So when I stand on both national and international stages, it's easy to have that conversation with them. I understand them, and they understand me. I have been where they are, have yelled the same words, and have shaken my head at the same things. I have been frustrated, unfulfilled, and insignificant too, but I chose to answer my purpose when it called to me, and now I am making an impact that will be felt for generations.

It's my mission to help the women in my world do the same thing. I love them like they were my mom or my sister or my best friend. Their vision is *my* vision, and I serve from that place. I cheer for them, I cry with them, and I share about them. I am completely sold on their significance. Whether I'm speaking to them, coaching with them, or they are reading some of my work, I want them to know that they are now a part of my world if they choose to be. I don't want the whole planet—I want them.

Who makes up your world? Please don't make the mistake of looking all over the *planet*. Undoubtedly, those who make up your world are just like you. Look around you. Pay attention. Who's been asking how you've done *this* or achieved *that*? They are who you are here to serve.

WHAT

Now that we've determined *who* you are here to serve, we need to determine *what* exactly you are serving. Once again, it's not about what you want. Your central focus should and must be this: *What does my audience want from me?* It doesn't matter what it is you want to give. Your audience will tell you what they want. You have to trust them and give them what they are asking for. This is why first determining *who* in the world you are here to serve is key. And because your world is probably made up of people just like you, it makes it easier to serve them.

As I alluded to earlier, in assessing your relationships and thinking through your audience, I'm confident that you will recall one or more points in time when someone asked you how you were able to accomplish a certain thing. Whether it was your attitude toward the achievement, the steps you took to get there, or how you managed life once you arrived to the breakthrough, they want to know what to do, and they need you to show and tell them. Do you think it would be difficult to create a way to do that? I don't think so because you've already lived it. You're an expert at it!

You probably had no idea that I could read minds, but that's one of my hidden talents. So I know right now you're thinking, "EXPERT? I'm no

EXPERT, Eboni! I just did something. I don't even think I did it well, let alone well enough to be called an expert!" I agree that "expert" can be a scary word, and many of the definitions out there for expert are really just assumptions. An expert is simply someone who has developed a skill because of their experience. Look it up. I'll wait...

Once, I was helping a client get clear on her *what*. We established that her *who* was mothers who wanted to establish a nonprofit entity. As we continued on the path to WHATville, I asked her, "What do you feel like you could teach these moms?" The expression on her face was priceless! She felt just like you—unqualified to share her significance because she wasn't an "expert." Seeing her expression, I immediately rephrased the question. Instead I asked her, "What were the steps you took to start your nonprofit from scratch?" She proceeded to rattle off all kinds of things, so much so that I almost couldn't keep up as I was writing notes down! Her confidence at that point in our conversation soared because she had already done this thing. She had conquered it so she was confident in her knowledge of what it took. When she was done, I looked at her and said, "THAT is what you're going to teach those mommies!" She was floored!

Part of our fear in agreeing that we are experts at a particular endeavor is because we are confident that there are others who know more about it than we do. Well, that *is* true. There are indeed lots of people who know more about what you know about. They have more knowledge, more practical application, and more people watching them and learning from them. (Stay with me here because although you may think I am proving your point, I'm not!) Although this is at the forefront of our thinking and is the source of our refusal to accept that we are experts in our areas of significance, there is one thing we fail to realize— there are others out there who do *not* have more knowledge, more practical application, or more people watching and learning from them than you do! Those are the individuals who make up your *world*. To them, YOU are the expert, and they need YOU to show them the way.

I serve my significance through my writing, coaching, and speaking. I am the solution for aspiring and current female entrepreneurs who yearn to trail blaze and play a more significant role in the world. My desire is to help them get clear on their mission, get clear on their message, and get clear on their money because what they're doing right now is nothing compared to what they are capable of doing. What are you going to do for, with, and/or about your audience?

WHEN

When should you start? That's a great question! Timing is indeed everything, but there is also no "right time" to begin. I know it sounds contradictory, so let me explain. You must avoid the quicksand of waiting. There are those who died an insignificant death because they were still waiting—on God, on the money, on the right connections, on the kids to grow up, on *something*. In actuality, they were only waiting on the one thing that actually matters—themselves. Most often, the only reason we don't move when we know we should is because we're waiting on ourselves. We are our own worst enemy and cruelest critic.

I'm reminded of a passage in my most favorite book in the world, the Bible. In one New Testament passage it shares how lepers asked the Messiah to heal them. Although at other times, He commanded on the spot for people to be healed, and they were, He took a different approach with this group. When the lepers asked for healing, he instructed them to go and show themselves to the priests in the city. This was interesting because in that time, lepers were forced to live outside the city due to their condition. There was a huge risk if they followed the instructions; at the least they'd be openly ridiculed, and at the most they'd be stoned to death. For Messiah to instruct them to go against societal (and health) norms was almost akin to suicide. It was incredibly bad timing! However, on His word, they turned and began walking toward their new destination. And the scripture says that "as they went," they were healed (Luke 17:14)! Two things happened here that I believe are critical in understanding your *when*. First, the lepers did not question the word they got. Messiah gave them the instruction and they immediately turned and began going. They understood that they were to go immediately. I imagine that somewhere in that moment, something about the Voice that gave the command gave them all the courage they needed. Did the lepers know what they risked by going into the city? Of course they did! But on the word *go*, they set out anyway. Their *when* was NOW.

Second, it was on the way to their healing that they actually received it. Did you catch that? *What they needed met them on their journey to it.* They weren't looking for healing; they were looking for the priests. "As they went," they were healed! I'd like to believe that somewhere in them, they knew that if they were obedient to the command to GO, they would at some point GET. The timing was not convenient. In fact, it was an incredibly precarious situation, however, that did not stop them. The passage does not say at what exact moment on their journey they received what they needed, but the key is in their obedience, their forward movement, and their decision to go. Someone in their party looked down at their hands or maybe at their legs and feet. Someone looked at the person next to them and dared touch one of their limbs. At some point someone screamed, I'm healed! I'm healed! and the rejoicing began. It happened *suddenly.* Suddenly, while they were doing what they were told, they received!

In my mind, this gives credence to the notion that there is never a *right* time—there is only time. We are only allotted a few hours of it each day. What you have to determine is whether you are going to spend it waiting for it to be *right*. What I believe I know about you is that you have heard the "GO," but some set of circumstances has told you otherwise. Now you are in a holding pattern. What's holding you? Is it fear, regret, past mistakes, rejection, doubt, or other people? WHAT IS IT?

What is it that is keeping you from living significantly?

The obvious answer to the "When?" question is NOW! It's said, "There's no time like the present," and when it comes to exposing your significance and giving it direction, I approve that message.

WHERE

The *where* of your significance is directly related to your *who* and your *what*. Just as Mother Teresa served her audience in the streets of Calcutta, there is a place where your *who* lives. This does not necessarily mean that you have to physically move to a new location, although that is entirely possible. What it means is that you have to be accessible to your audience and vice versa. You also have to be privy to the needs of your audience. The delivery depends on your *what*. Sometimes it will require you to go to where your audience is. Other times, you may be able to be in one, static location, and your tribe comes to you through some means. Mother Teresa lived among the people she served, but you may be able to use your laptop and Wi-Fi connection to successfully reach those you are here to serve—the Internet and social media have made our world much smaller.

Get creative! Your audience's ability to be in close proximity to your message and those you serve is vital to creating a legendary life and death. As we've discussed, you have to be seen, heard, and followed. This will be virtually impossible if those you serve do not know where you are or how to find you. Time to come out of hiding. Where will you serve your significance?

HOW

This is the question that I get asked most often from my coaching clients—the question of *how*. Hold on to your seat because I am going to give you the same answer I give them, and it will shock you—I don't have any earthly idea how you're going to do this! Truth be told (and I coach my clients on this too), the *how* really doesn't matter much at all. Your methods will always have to change based on the times, who you serve your significance, and many other dynamics. What's important is going with the flow of the obvious. Just like your *when*, the how will never be completely perfect. Your plan will have glitches. It may fall through many times. If your plan includes other humans, it will most definitely hit a snag on occasion. If you focus on having a perfect *how*, you'll sit in the valley of indecision again. Remember the quicksand of waiting?

I personally believe that taking action in the most obvious direction at the time is more effective than attempting to create a fail-safe, foolproof plan. I want to be clear and say that I'm not suggesting that you don't plan at all. What I am saying is that you cannot afford to stop moving forward because you're waiting to build the perfect plan. Likewise, you cannot afford to sit down on your purpose because what you thought was a perfect plan turned out not to be. Your *how* is a by-product of your action.

The process usually begins with an idea. As you've been reading and recording your insights, you have had a few light bulbs go off in your head. Already, you've gotten some inclination of a plan of sorts—a *how*. Right now, in this moment, what is it that you could DO to put you one step closer to living your significance out loud? There is always something. What is that action step for you? Go ahead and do it! What's cool is that as you're in the midst of taking that step, the next one becomes a little bit more obvious. The *how* becomes a little bit more obvious. There is something about action that creates more action. Remember Newton's First

Law of Motion: an object in motion tends to remain in motion. But remember, my friend, the converse is true as well: an object at rest tends to remain at rest. Haven't you rested enough?

WHY

There are moments on my legendary journey that I lack emotional fortitude. A desire to be normal or "regular" as I sometimes call it, routs me. For a split second, I no longer want the responsibility that living significantly immediately requires. Sometimes this happens because I lose focus. Other times, it is because I am intently focused on the wrong thing. Our *why* is synonymous with our *who* and our *what*. Remaining focused on your *why* will do wonders for your emotional and mental stamina. It is incredibly easy to get sidetracked and then disgruntled because our focus has shifted to something other than what's really important. Should your focus remain off, despair will soon follow, and you'll be enticed to give up. That subtle but distracting desire to be "regular" will take the opportunity to creep in.

It will be enticing to compare your journey with others or to complain about what is not going right. The world—and the graveyard—is filled with "regular folks" because it's much easier to sit on the porch than to take your place among the big dogs. It's much easier to sit than it is to run. I know that a lack of focus causes Lazyboy™ recliners to suddenly manifest. It's quite bizarre actually!

Likewise, it will be tempting to consider what other people are *not* saying or doing. Let's be clear: everyone will not acknowledge your work. In fact, most people won't, primarily because they are not who you are here to serve anyway. You must keep that in mind—those you serve are the ones that matter. I want to take a moment here on this subject and offer some advice: for the sake of everyone's sanity, please let your family off the hook! This may be a heartbreaker for some and a point of contention for others, but it is necessary for all. Too often we hold our family members hostage to our dreams and our purpose. Unfortunately, we believe that they should be and are as invested in our success as we are. And while it is ideal for everyone in our family, especially our immediate family, to buy into our significance, the reality is that most will not. This phenomenon occurs, not because they don't believe that you are significant, but rather, they don't know this *new and improved* you. To them, you will always be "(insert your childhood nickname)." Will they be proud? Probably. Will they tell others about what you do? More than likely. Will they invest financially? Don't count on it. If they do, awesome! If they don't, awesome! That just means they are not your audience. They don't live in your world, and that's okay.

What I can guarantee is these moments that call you off track will occur often. What will keep us both going is to remember our *why*. In those times, I think of the women I serve. I go back and watch their testimonial videos or read through a text or email they've sent me. Over the years, there have been many who have thanked me for doing what I do and being who I am. (This is why it is crucial that your significance be measurable.) They keep going because I do. I also think about my sons and the security they have knowing that Mommy living her significance also helps to pay the bills. I think about how I am an example to them of what's possible when you are sold on your own value. But more than anything else, I begin to reflect on what life was like when I was *insignificant*. Although it took a car accident to shake me into the revelation that I didn't matter, I am no less grateful for the wake-up call. Is the frustration and the bitterness that insignificance causes really worth it? Think back through the work we've done so far. To have read this far, you must be committed to something. To what is that commitment attached? My prayer is that your commitment and resolve hinge on the truth that you are significant, and now others need to know that as well.

"But Eboni, how am I supposed to do all this stuff? How am I supposed to get all this done? You don't just all of a sudden become significant and important!" First, let me just acknowledge that I heard you ask those questions about two pages ago, so I was prepared. Second, I want to reiterate that the work we're doing is not to *make* you significant and important. The reality is that you are *already* significant and important. You want proof? Put your hand on your chest. Do you feel that continuous beating? There's your proof. The role of this book is to help you understand that reality and give you steps to live it out so that you won't remain a well-kept secret. That, my friend, is a good reason *why*.

SIGNIFICANT QUESTIONS

Who lives in your world? Who is it that you are here to serve your significance for?

_____

_____

_____

What do the people in your world want from you?

_____

_____

_____

How do you know?

_____

_____

At what are you an expert? What is that *something* that people always ask you about and want to know the *how* behind?

_____

_____

What were the steps you took to accomplish it?

1. _____

2. _____

3. _____

4. _____

5. _____

What are you to serve to those you are called to?

_____

_____

What is it that is keeping you from living significantly right now?

_____

_____

_____

How will you overcome this?

_____

_____

_____

Where will you serve your significance?

_____

_____

_____

Right now, in this moment, what is it that you could DO to put you one step closer to living your significance out loud?

_____

_____

_____

What is Your Evidence?

A life well lived leaves clues

In November 2014, after spending the greater part of the evening at an I Am Woman Network BizLive Birmingham event, I arrived home later than usual. As soon as I walked in the door, my husband frantically beckoned me to join him in our home office. He was at his laptop with a look of dismay on his face. As I rounded the corner to see what the matter was, I saw it. A newsflash announcing that Dr. Myles Munroe, world-renowned speaker, author, humanitarian, dignitary, and pastor, was dead. Dead. *Gone*. The shock almost caused me to double over. Surely this was some cruel and evil Internet prank. In silence, I walked to my bedroom and fell down across my bed. I was completely and utterly dumbfounded. My husband joined me not long after. We both just kind of looked at each other. After several minutes, we asked aloud all the questions we had already been thinking. We tried to figure out why this had happened and tried to discern who may have been to blame. It felt like Dr. Myles had been *stolen* from us. I was so grateful to be lying next to my husband that night. I needed to feel safe.

Dr. Myles Munroe was dead. His wife, Ruth, was gone as well. He and several members of his staff, including his youth pastor, the youth pastor's pregnant wife, and their young son, were all killed in a horrific plane crash. To say that I was *sad* is a gross understatement. I cried many, many times. I was shattered. I was devastated to the point of being almost physically ill. Even now, as I think about him being gone, my heart becomes heavy. It felt as if my own father had died. I was sick about it. In the days that followed, I would scour social media for updates on the state of his children and the ministry he left behind. And although I have watched him online over and over again throughout the years, I devoured all of his YouTube videos, not taking notes this time, but just trying to get one more glimpse of this man whose gift helped to mold me into the woman that I am. This man whose ministry had given substance to my desire to serve.

What I know about Dr. Myles is that he seized every opportunity. Every time he was given the chance, he lived *on* purpose and *with* purpose. In fact, his message concerning purpose—what it is, how to find it, and where it comes from—has had global impact. Although it was decades ago that he arrived on the scene with the message of purpose and vision, this message is still being "discovered" by millions today! Very early in his life, Dr. Myles made the decision to intentionally live and to live intentionally. He always talked about "dying empty," having poured all of your gifts and talents into others. He made the choice to be significant.

I began to take inventory of my life again. Similar to when I could have lost my own life in that car accident, I was now thinking about his life that was now over because of an accident. At the time of Dr. Myles' death, it had been six years since my son and I had flipped in my SUV and walked away from it. Just as I did after the car accident, I again forced myself to ask some tough questions and face some even tougher realities. And just as before, I reviled my answers to my own questions. Since that time, had I truly been honoring my own personal significance as I had vowed to do not long after the accident? How many opportunities had I passed on because I failed to agree that I was worthy of them? What plans had I considered too risky because of a fear of success? What had I *not* accomplished because I had lost focus? How many dreams were on life support because of my refusal to breathe life into them?

You may be thinking that I must have been close to Dr. Myles to react in the way that I did. Surely he was my personal mentor or, at the very least, I must have met him in person. What's interesting is that none of that is true. I had never met Dr. Myles in person. I had never attended his events or even been to a conference where he was speaking. Not once had I seen him in person. I had never been to the church he founded, Bahamas Faith Ministries International, in Nassau. I had only "met" him through his numerous books, CDs, tapes, and videos. I had been following him and his ministry since I was a teenager, getting my first exposure through my mom. For years, it had been my desire to meet him and to be mentored by him. In fact, I had planned to be at his conference in the Bahamas that November—the same conference he was headed to when the plane crashed. Another one of those missed opportunities.

While he lived, Dr. Myles inspired me to be greater, and he continued to do so in his death. I had never met nor seen him in person, yet both Dr. Myles Munroe's life and his death called me to the carpet. They impacted me immensely. I want you to notice I said *both* his life *and* his death. That is the goal. For you and I both to create lives that, when *we* die, will cause people to not only reminisce, but to also reassess their lives, their journey, and their own personal significance. *A life well lived leaves clues.* What is *your* evidence?

Dr. Myles' life has left us with step five—the will and desire to rule and lead (dominate) in your area of significance. Dr. Myles' teachings stand out in my mind as being focused on two areas: Kingdom and leadership. He was a master at interweaving the principles of both, whether he was speaking in a sacred or secular environment. He owned those principles, that message, of Kingdom and leadership. In fact, he dominated in the space so much so that pastors, speakers, leaders, CEOs, and the like not only sought him out for his knowledge and wisdom, but they have taught his principles to their own spheres of influence! Dr. Myles Munroe was the front-runner in his area of significance. You must be as well.

There are four areas in which your significance must dominate:

- Your dedication
- Your conversation

- Your association

- Your monetization

DEDICATION

When he was younger, my husband was a tremendous fan of Tupac Shakur. Even today, if a Tupac song comes on, he'll bob his head and attempt to rap along with the song. Tupac was another individual gone too soon, but he commanded the attention in his area of significance while he was alive and continues to do so even after his death. He had a song called "Against All Odds," and while I don't suggest you go listen to it if you're not already familiar (lots of language that you may find objectionable), I do want you to get the premise. When you dominate in your significance, you must do so against ALL odds, amidst every obstacle, without any backing, and for all the right reasons.

First, there will be moments when you will have to fight for your significance. There will be both internal and external battles, but you must have an "against all odds" dedication to the pursuit and the manifestation of your purpose. Much of the work we've done here will have prepared you for the internal struggle. However, there will also be external battles that must be fought and won. There will be people who won't like your new determination. There will be situations that you will encounter that will hinder you. Your body will sometimes fatigue, or you will lack the physical stamina to serve.

As I said earlier, this is when you must remember your *why* and rededicate yourself to your significance. Self-care will also be vital for your continued dedication. Those who serve others, especially us women who serve others, are most often guilty of putting everything before ourselves. We work and serve to create a home for our families, put clothing on the backs of our children, be a valuable member of the team at work, and be effective in ministry at our houses of worship—these are all things we do to hold the world around us together. During some point in human history, we women were told that to be self-sacrificing and self-deprecating was somehow a defining and honorable characteristic of women. I say not so. The tomfoolery that is being "all things to all people" and then waiting on someone to return the favor is why women become depressed, overlooked, stressed out, and broken down. Further, that brand of tomfoolery will also not lead to a significant life. More likely, it will lead to an early (and insignificant) death.

Being dedicated to, and at intervals rededicating to, your own significance means you understand that although you are serving others, *you* are still central; without you there is no service. Consequently, you have to be just as dedicated to taking care of yourself—spirit, soul, and body—as you are to taking care of those you serve your significance to. Every so often, go to the spa, take a vacation, treat yourself to your favorite meal, or buy that expensive purse. Likewise, eat healthy, drink water, enjoy some type of physical activity every day, pray, and meditate. Do whatever it takes to show some appreciation to *you* for the work that you do to serve your *world*. Against ALL odds, be dedicated to the truth that you are necessary and important.

Second, you must be dedicated to those you serve. For some, serving their significance will mean they will be in a position to offer paid products, services, opportunities, and the like (we'll talk more about this a little later). I believe that everyone should do this on some level, and it's what I speak about and coach on. I don't know if it will be the case for you my friend, but if it is, be sure to monitor your emotions, your actions, and your desires.

At the point that you begin creating any modicum of income from your significance, you may become tempted to turn all your energies toward making more money. While this is fine in theory, it can quickly produce what I call "Dollar Sign Vision." If your wealth is the result of you serving your significance well (because people will pay for what they value), then that's fine. But if you begin to become more dedicated to making money than you are to making a difference, your house of cards will soon crumble. The only person interested in making you rich is you. When you develop dollar signs in your eyes, it means you have lost sight of what's genuinely important—your *who*. In short order, your audience will get the notion of your true heart's desire, and they will leave you to yourself.

CONVERSATION

What are you saying about yourself and your significance? When you talk about who you are and what you are here to do, does your conversation agree with your significance? Can you share how you are "the bomb dot com" at being you and doing what you do without feeling bad about it? Further, can you achieve that level of confidence without allowing other people to make you feel bad about it? When you dominate in your area of significance, you have no apprehension about talking about it humbly. There is nothing wrong with making known your expertise and your value. Too often, we confuse confidence with arrogance. Arrogance is an attitude of superiority that causes you to look down on others. That is completely different from being conscious of your personal power and your abilities because you choose to operate in that power. That's what confidence is. When you dominate in your area of significance, confidence and humility dwell in the same house.

A word of caution: be careful to avoid false humility. I'm sure you've experienced someone who wanted you to believe that they were humble when in actuality they weren't. Is it as irritating to you as it is to me? Out of their mouths they consistently say that they are not seeking any glory for themselves, but their actions tell a much different story. False humility is simply pride in disguise. The usual voice of pride wants to be sure you hear them and see them. They prefer to have the credit. A person who wants you to believe that he or she is humble wants the same, but they want it to come from *you* so that their pride won't be so obvious. They continually share how they don't want the glory because they want to hear *you* say how much they should have it!

False humility does nothing to serve your significance. It does more to undermine your significance than it does to bolster it. Further, false humility is a tool of the insecure. Those who are insecure are not completely sold on their significance. This is evident by their need for validation from others. Whether the expression of that need is overt or covert, the culprit is still the same: insecurity. When you do what you are supposed to be doing for those you are designed and destined to be doing it with and for, influence and ascendency is inevitable. You don't have to try to coax people into telling you that you're doing the doggone thang! That is why it is absolutely imperative that you be your own biggest fan. That you dedicate yourself to your *who* and also to *you* so that your conversation conveys those ideals to everyone you serve. You will never dominate in your area of significance otherwise.

ASSOCIATION

We've discussed before about how you have no other choice but to play in a "bigger room" if you expect to create a legendary life and death. When you command influence in your area of significance, your room changes automatically.

There will be some rooms that you request to be a part of, but there will be many others that you are invited into because you are living out loud. A by-product of this phenomenon is that, more than likely, you will transition from your "old crew" and be included in bigger endeavors than what you had in the past. If your "old crew" is not made up of individuals who celebrate you, be wary—jealousy and envy are usually not far behind. Fortunately, the great majority of my circle has been made up of those who take pleasure in watching me succeed. However, that has not always been the case.

I received a phone call one morning from a woman who had considered me a close friend. I knew from the tone of her voice and the time of the call that she was feeling disdain of some sort. During her conversation she accused me of thinking of myself as "better" than others (namely herself) and that I acted as if I had reached some sort of higher status than those around me. I listened closely to what was being said, but also made it a point to discern what was *not* being said. Because we were both a part of the same community of women at the time, I asked if she had been present during a meeting that had occurred just days earlier, during which I poured my heart out, asking for prayer because I was in desperate need. She had not been present. I therefore felt compelled to explain that in no way did I believe I was more capable, more important, or more virtuous than anyone else. Quite the contrary—at that point in my life, I felt like I was a complete and utter failure. She was quiet.

As the conversation progressed, the real reason for her hurt and anger was revealed—she was jealous and felt left out. In her mind, she had imagined that we would live out our significance together. She depended heavily on me to draw out of her the wealth of abundance that is in her. However, what she didn't factor in was a change in my associations. I learned from raising the level of my associations that neither the onus nor the responsibility were on me to ensure that she live her greatness. That choice belongs to each of us, and I could not make that choice for her. I had made it for myself, and it was beginning to show. I was beginning to make a mark, and people were noticing my path of creating influence and the legacy I am to leave. She did not like that I was doing it without her.

When you associate higher and serve in a bigger room, people will accuse you of changing. Don't go the way of self-deprecation and fight for a lower position. Admit that you have changed and celebrate that! Truth be told, they should also be celebrating the fact that you've changed. Taking control of your life and taking back your future should not be cause or reason for apology. It also should not be a tool for others to use against you to hurt you. When you dominate in your area of significance, you become an example for others who don't yet know that they can as well. I believe there is honor in that. The dishonor comes when you succumb to the pressure of others to be less than who you are because it makes *them* more comfortable with their insignificance. No, my friend. Refuse to diminish yourself and your significance! Do not allow their issues to become yours. Associate higher. Find a bigger room and deliberately have a seat in it. When you dominate in that sphere of influence, find the next larger sphere and dominate in that one as well. Your *who* needs to be able to follow the trail that you blaze.

MONETIZATION

To monetize means to take something of value and use it to generate income. I mentioned earlier about how it is possible to be paid for your significance. I enjoy the freedom that living significantly has afforded me, but I have been able to create that freedom because I have chosen to monetize my significance and my value. Now before you pick up a stone and accuse me of some moral flaw, allow me to put what I'm saying into perspective. Athletes, celebrities, government officials, CEOs of corporations, and many others are all paid (most times handsomely) for their significance. They earn some amount of money in exchange for their wisdom, ability, talent, expertise, and function. As a result, they are able to command influence in their respective areas, and their influence usually crosses over into other platforms as well. (Dr. Myles is a perfect example of this.) They become the innovators, the change agents, and the decision makers. You need to be in that same position of influence and ability. Therefore, the conclusion is obvious—you must monetize your significance in some way.

Money has no morals. In error, we tend to attach morals to dollar bills, but that is erroneous. An illegal drug dealer's money is no less moral than a pastor's. Money is amoral, which is why it needs to be in the hands of those who understand what it means to serve their *who* genuinely, diligently, and effectively. The function of money is determined by the morals of the one who possesses it. I share that because you may have some apprehension about monetizing your significance. For some, it feels sleazy or hypocritical to accept payment for their expertise. If that is you, I would suggest you quit your job. You are being a hypocrite by allowing them to pay you for your expertise and ability.

Forgive my sarcasm, but it is the truth. What's worse though is that those same individuals who fear hypocrisy would quit their job in a heartbeat if they felt they really could get paid for their significance! Most people abhor their jobs because they are not fulfilled in them. Why? They now realize that their employ is the cage of their significance. The most handsome reward we can receive in life is to be able to be paid for what we were born to do and who we were born to be. In reality, when you dominate in your area of significance, it's impossible to be broke. To reiterate an earlier statement, people will pay for what they value. The more value you bring, the more people will pay.

Are you in a position right now to leave a financial inheritance to your posterity? I don't mean the money you have stashed under your mattress or buried under the tree outside. I also don't mean the money you *intended* to save. I am referring to whether or not you have a diversified portfolio that, when you die, will have a positive financial impact. Or, will your loved ones be left with your debt and the dream of getting out of it that you never realized? This is another reason for me to challenge you to monetize your greatness. You cannot die and your posterity not have the financial means to continue your legacy. No matter how legendary you are in death, it will not last if the money to fund the change you created is not available. Monetizing your significance (and teaching your children to do the same) will help to solidify your legacy.

SIGNIFICANT QUESTIONS

Think of someone you greatly admire. What "clues" has their life left for you to find?

_____

_____

_____

In what ways has this person made the choice to be significant?

_____

_____

_____

Has their decision to live significantly impacted you?   Yes   No

Why not or how so?

_____

_____

_____

What **current** evidence do you have of "a life well lived" (one that has been lived significantly)?

_____

_____

_____

What does it mean to "dominate in your area of significance"?

_____

_____

Are you willing to do what it takes to dominate?
　　Yes　　No

Will you have an "against ALL odds" dedication?
　　Yes　　No

How will you integrate self-care in your pursuit?

_____

_____

_____

What mental and emotional boundaries can you put in place now that will feed your dedication to your *who* and avoid "Dollar Sign Vision"?

_____

_____

_____

What have you been saying about yourself and your significance?

_____

_____

Has your conversation conveyed the fact that you are important and necessary on the planet?

    Yes   No

If not, will you adjust your conversation to match your significance and importance on the earth?

    Yes   No

Taking an honest assessment, have you been falsely humble in your interactions with others?

    Yes   No

If yes, what is the source of your insecurities?

_____

_____

What mental and emotional boundaries will you put in place to overcome the insecurity?

_____

_____

_____

What fears do you have about that transition?

_____

_____

_____

Do you believe you can monetize your significance? Yes   No

If no, why not?

_____

_____

Does monetizing your expertise seem immoral to you?   Yes   No

Why not or how so?

_____

_____

_____

Are you willing to monetize your message and your significance?   Yes   No

What are some ways you could do that?

_____

_____

_____

The Man in the Mirror

"I'm starting with the man in the mirror. I'm asking him to change his ways." – Michael Jackson

Throughout this journey of finding and relishing in your significance factor, I have included moments and areas of self-reflection and self-assessment. Both are vital as you continue further on this journey to living a legendary life and a lasting legacy. As such, I want to leave you with one last activity. When I speak on stages all across the country, this activity is the one that tends to leave the greatest impression on listeners. Feel free to complete it now, but make time to complete it often, at reasonable but specific intervals. Use it as a gut check—a system to keep you accountable to living your significance out loud.

The Mirror

When I am conducting this activity with a live audience, I ask them to use their hand in front of their face as their makeshift "mirror." I am going to ask you to do the same. However, if possible, I'm going to ask that you do one better—if you are near an actual mirror or can get near one, do that! Even your makeup compact will do. It will make this activity that much more effective and powerful.

Step #1

Look in the mirror and ask yourself this question:

Who are you?

Give yourself time to hear the answer and then make a note of it.

Step #2

Look in the mirror again and ask yourself:

What do you stand for?

Again, give yourself time to hear the response and then make a note of it.

Step #3

Look in the mirror one last time and ask yourself this final question:

What is your most recent evidence of it?

Remember to give yourself time to hear the response and then make a note of it.

This activity will keep you grounded. It allows you to "prove" to yourself that you are who you say you are and that you truly stand for what you say you stand for. When you are convinced of it yourself, it's much easier to live it out. Remember, the tongue in your mouth must match the tongue in your shoe.

Power of Agreement

"The good person produces good things from the store of good in his heart, while the evil person produces evil things from the store of evil in his heart. For his mouth speaks what overflows from his heart." – Luke 6:45 CJB

We talked before about how what you say must match what you believe. Your conversation and your belief must be congruent if you expect to have a legendary life and death. Until that happens, nothing else will.

Here are a series of declarations that will help you in that endeavor. Even if the circumstances around you don't match what you are declaring, do not let that deter you. Just as your significance must be *lived* out loud, so must what you say about your significance be *said* out loud. Make these declarations every day so that they become a part of you. The goal is for you to truly believe what you are declaring. Therefore, these should become your automatic responses instead of any negative things you've been saying until this point. Oh, and by the way, it doesn't matter if no one else believes it yet—as long as you do!

- I declare that I am legendary! I live a life that is impacting, action-filled, and service-oriented.

- I declare that I am significant! My life matters and so will my death. I will be *more* in life so that I can be *more* in death as well.

- I declare that my gift makes room for me and places me in front of individuals of influence and power!

- I declare that every day, God causes someone to use their power, their ability, their influence, and their resources to help me.

- I declare that every day, God allows me to use my power, my ability, my influence, and my resources to help someone else.

- I declare that as I go forward in my pursuit, I have everything I need to do everything I need to do.

- I declare that my capacity is increased to do and to be more today than I was yesterday.

- I declare that I have access to everything that God desires to do in my life.

- I declare that today I have permission to accomplish my ordained mission and goals. I have permission to pursue purpose.

- I declare that I have extraordinary faith and patience. I am aligned with others who are perfecting those areas as well so that I may obtain all that is destined for me.

- I declare that I am the person that I am supposed to be! I have faith in the "me" that I was born to be.

- I declare that I have new eyes to see opportunities, and the mental, spiritual, and emotional preparation to overcome opposition.

- I declare that as I commit to and live my significance to its full potential, God will provide the place to maximize it.

- I declare my refusal to settle for a life that is mediocre and characterized by limitations and restrictions.

- I declare that I expect to do mighty exploits. I do great things!

- I declare that I am prepared for greatness, power, and uncommon success.

- I declare that I will always speak the truth, exemplify the truth, uphold the truth, stand on the truth, and live the truth.

- I declare that I am realigned with my purpose and my personal authenticity.

- I declare that I am among those to whom the capacity to receive has been given.

ABOUT THE AUTHOR

Described as engaging, anointed, powerful, fiery, and hilarious, Eboni L. Truss is passionate about helping women discover and claim their most fulfilling professional and personal lives.

As an empowerment speaker and bestselling author, Eboni's focus is leading her clients to be impact-centered entrepreneurs. Through her "Circle of Significance" (COS) mentorship program, she empowers participants to grow, progress, and achieve their desired goals. She also speaks and writes about designing broader and bolder lifestyles, often using her book *The Significance Factor* as a foundational guide.

A formally trained relationship builder and educator, Eboni graduated from Talladega College, the "Harvard of the South," with a Bachelor's in Sociology. She later earned a Master's in Elementary Education from the University of Phoenix. Though born and raised in Detroit, she currently lives in Talladega with her husband and two sons. And when she isn't wearing one of her many business hats, she's probably couponing, vacationing, volunteering, or watching Shark Tank with the family.

To find out all the ways in which Eboni serves her significance to her world and how she can serve you too, visit www.EboniTruss.com to schedule a "Discovery Session" with her, as well as download the free gift she has available just for you!

FABULOUS NEW LIFE

28 Women:
Boldly Sharing
Their Transformational
Journey to Creating
an Extraordinary Life

Aprille Franks-Hunt
Eboni L. Truss, Co-Author

Fabulous New Life is the best-selling anthology of real life stories from 28 women around the United States who have overcome harrowing odds. Compiled by thought leader, Aprille Franks-Hunt, the contributors share with the readers their joy, triumphs and lessons in hopes to inspire other women to live a more extraordinary life.

Get your copy at:
www.EboniTruss.com/Fabulous-New-Life

Keep Going in the Direction of Greatness!

www.TheSignificanceFactor.com

Join The Significance Factor Community and get the resources to stay committed to your journey of living your significance out loud!

Small group activities

Book tour dates and locations

The *official* "Legendary" blinged out t-shirt

Testimonials

The Significance Factor Conference:
"Mission, Message, Money"

The "Circle of Significance" Mentorship Program

Get the tools necessary to NOT be "just another obituary"!

WE WANT TO HEAR FROM YOU!!!

If this book has made a difference in your life Eboni would be delighted to hear about it.
Leave a review on Amazon.com!

BOOK EBONI TO SPEAK AT YOUR NEXT EVENT!
Send an email to: booking@publishyourgift.com

Learn more about Eboni at:
www.EboniTruss.com

FOLLOW EBONI ON SOCIAL MEDIA

 EboniLTruss    EboniTruss

---

"EMPOWERING YOU TO IMPACT GENERATIONS"
WWW.PUBLISHYOURGIFT.COM